AF228852

XTREME SNAKES
COPPERHEADS

BY S.L. HAMILTON

A&D Xtreme
An imprint of Abdo Publishing | abdopublishing.com

abdopublishing.com

Published by Abdo Publishing, a division of ABDO, PO Box 398166, Minneapolis, Minnesota 55439. Copyright ©2019 by Abdo Consulting Group, Inc. International copyrights reserved in all countries. No part of this book may be reproduced
in any form without written permission from the publisher. A&D Xtreme™
is a trademark and logo of Abdo Publishing.

Printed in China.
022018
092018

Editor: John Hamilton
Copy Editor: Bridget O'Brien
Graphic Design: Sue Hamilton
Cover Design: Candice Keimig and Pakou Moua
Cover Photo: iStock
Interior Photos & Illustrations: Alamy-pgs 12-13, 18, 19, 20-21, 22-23, 24-25 & 30-31; Galileo Ramos-pgs 6-7 (upper); iStock-pgs 1, 2-3, 4-5, 7 (inset), 26 & 27; Kevin Fleming-pgs 8-9; Science Source-pgs 10-11, 14-15, 16-17, 28-29 & 32; Shutterstock-pgs 6-7 (lower).

Library of Congress Control Number: 2017963893
Publisher's Cataloging-in-Publication Data
Names: Hamilton, S.L., author.
Title: Copperheads / by S.L. Hamilton.
Description: Minneapolis, Minnesota : Abdo Publishing, 2019. |
    Series: Xtreme snakes | Includes online resources and index.
Identifiers: ISBN 9781532116018 (lib.bdg.) | ISBN 9781532156946 (ebook)
Subjects: LCSH: Copperhead--Juvenile literature. | Poisonous snakes--Juvenile
    literature. | Snakes--Juvenile literature. | Reptiles--Juvenile literature. |
    Herpetology--Juvenile literature.
Classification: DDC 597.963--dc23

CONTENTS

Copperheads

Copperheads are named for the penny-like color of their heads. There are five species of copperheads. They are native to the United States and Mexico. If you are bitten by a snake, it could very well be a copperhead. More copperhead bites are recorded every year than any other snake.

XTREME FACT – Copperhead venom is mild compared to other venomous snakes. They rarely kill something as big as an adult human.

BODY PARTS

The copperhead's scientific name is *Agkistrodon contortrix*. The words mean "fishhook" (fangs) and "twisted" (the pattern on the snake's body).

Hollow, needle-like fangs that fold up against the roof of the mouth when not in use.

Separate lower jaw sections allow the mouth to open wide over prey.

Nostril
Pit Organ
Copperheads have eyes with vertical pupils, like most venomous snakes. Non-venomous snakes usually have round pupils.
A copperhead has pit organs that detect heat given off by prey. The snake can "see" its victim, even when the prey doesn't move.

Tail
Ribs
Light yellow or green tail tip, usually found on young copperheads.

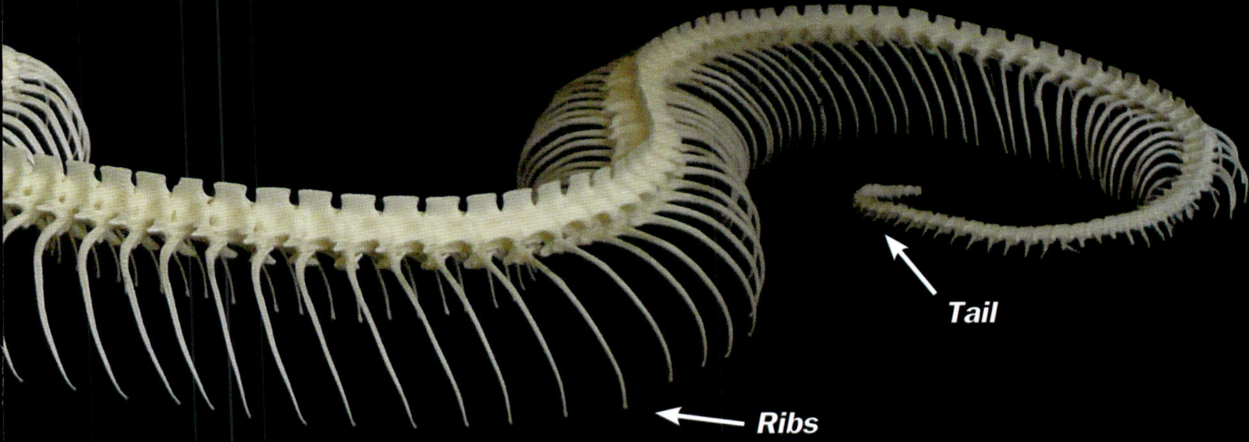

FANGS AND VENOM

Copperhead snakes have an unlimited number of fangs and other teeth. When one falls out, another replaces it. Copperheads lose their teeth frequently. A tooth may break off or stick in struggling prey. If this happens, there is another tooth behind it waiting to grow in.

Copperhead venom flows through the snake's hollow fangs and into its victim. The venom causes immediate pain at the bite site. The snake will hold smaller prey while the venom takes effect and its victim dies. Larger prey is bitten and let loose. The copperhead will track down its run-away victim and eat it later.

 PREY AND HUNTING

Copperheads are pit vipers. They use heat-seeking sensors called pit organs to find prey. They "see" the warmth given off by rodents, squirrels, birds, rabbits, and bats. Copperheads are patient. They wait for prey to get close, and then ambush them.

A copperhead uses its teeth to pull its prey into its mouth.

Copperheads also like cold-blooded meals. They eat frogs, toads, and lizards. Large insects are a tasty lunch, too. They are known to eat millipedes, dragonflies, cicadas, grasshoppers, and mantises. A copperhead will eat over twice its body weight in prey each year.

HABITAT

There are five species of copperheads. They live in the United States and Mexico. They include:
1) Southern Copperheads
2) Northern Copperheads
3) Broad-Banded Copperheads
4) Trans-Pecos Copperheads
5) Osage Copperheads

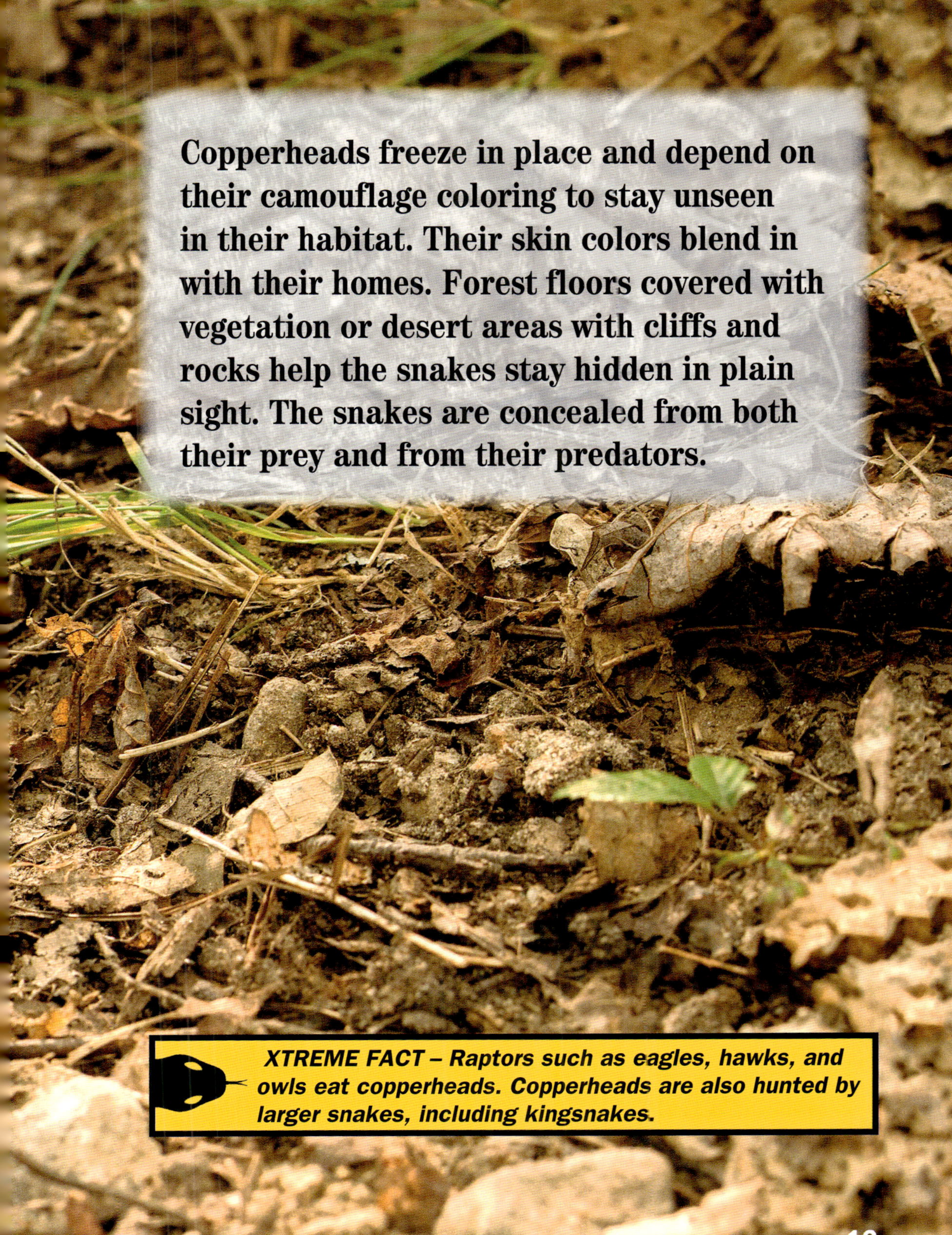

Copperheads freeze in place and depend on their camouflage coloring to stay unseen in their habitat. Their skin colors blend in with their homes. Forest floors covered with vegetation or desert areas with cliffs and rocks help the snakes stay hidden in plain sight. The snakes are concealed from both their prey and from their predators.

NESTING

Like most reptiles, copperheads begin life in an egg. However, a mother copperhead does not lay eggs. The eggs hatch inside the mother. She gives birth to a clear sac with about 4 to 8 live young inside. This is called being "ovoviviparous."

The young then break through the sac and take their first breaths. Babies are born ready to hunt. They have fangs, venom, and all the senses needed to find prey. This is important because copperhead mothers do not stay with their young.

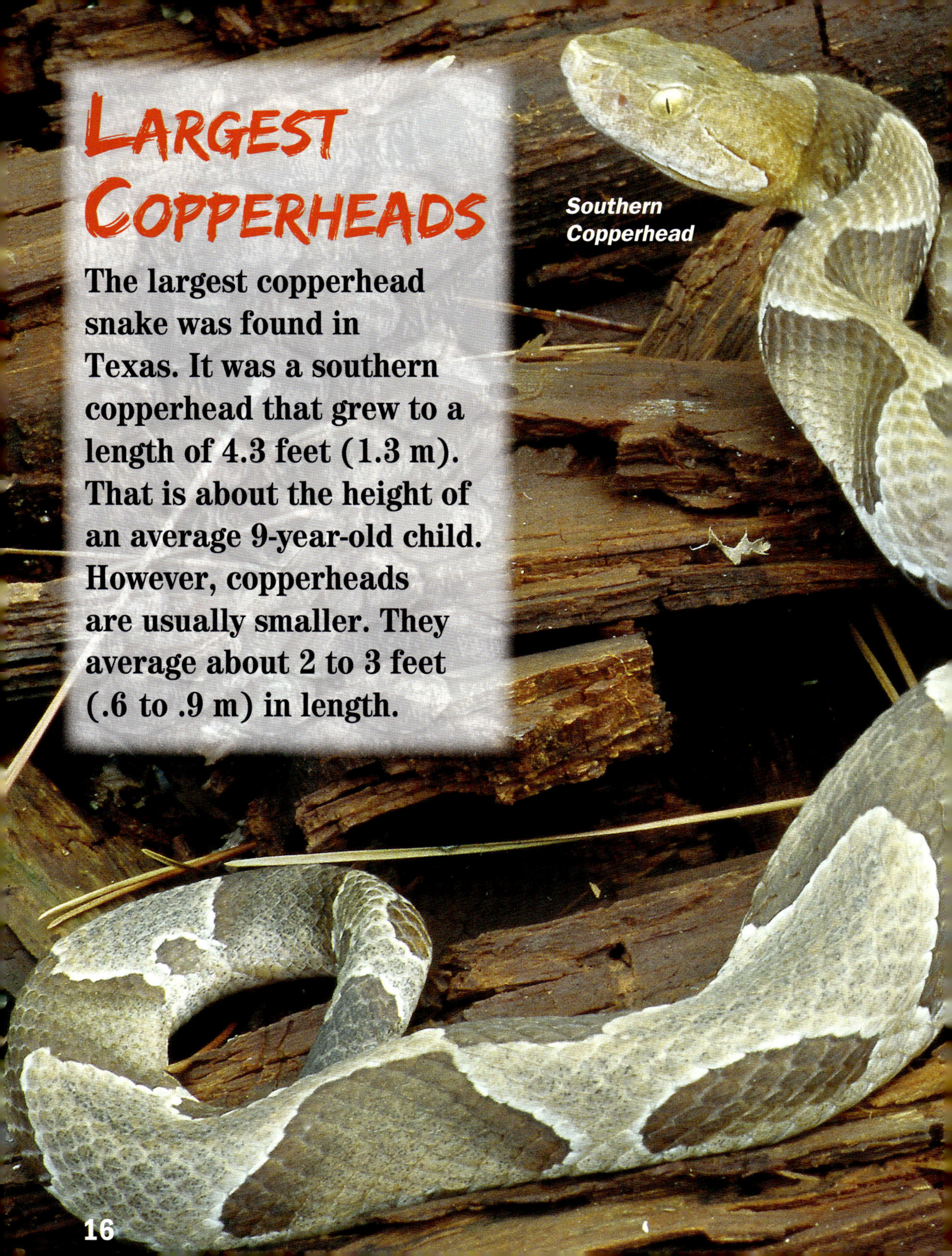

LARGEST COPPERHEADS

The largest copperhead snake was found in Texas. It was a southern copperhead that grew to a length of 4.3 feet (1.3 m). That is about the height of an average 9-year-old child. However, copperheads are usually smaller. They average about 2 to 3 feet (.6 to .9 m) in length.

Smallest Copperheads

The smallest copperheads are broad-banded and Trans-Pecos copperheads. They grow to a size of 2 to 3 feet (.6 to .9 m). Even these smaller copperheads deliver a venomous, painful bite.

If threatened, a copperhead will coil up and then raise its head, ready to strike. Their venom is a hemotoxin. This means it destroys red blood cells. Once bitten, a person will experience pain, tingling, swelling, and damage to muscle and bone tissue. Even the venom from small copperheads is very dangerous.

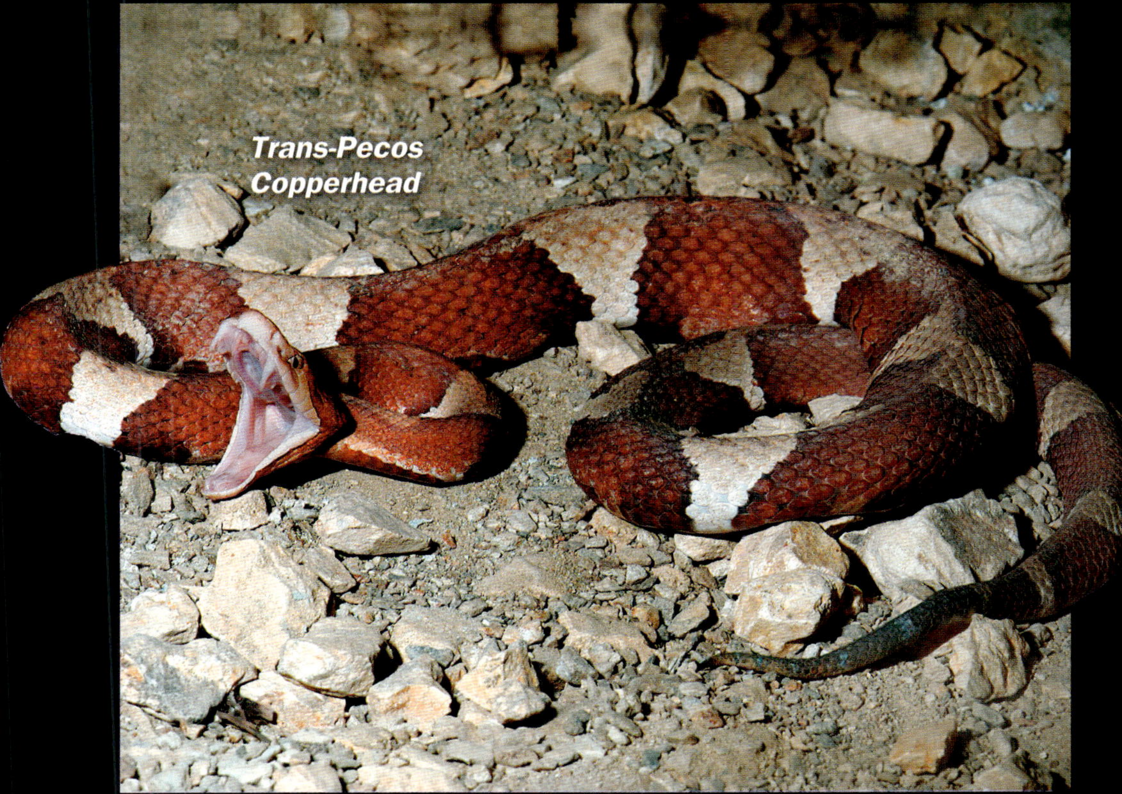

FASTEST STRIKER

All species of copperheads are quick to bite. And since they are very common snakes that slither into yards, garages, gardens, and woodpiles, they are often near to humans.

Southern Copperhead

XTREME FACT – Copperheads do not have a warning tail rattle. They do, however, shake their tails when threatened. Some give off an odor that smells musky.

Copperheads try to stay hidden by remaining motionless, but that makes it harder for people to see them. It's easy to step near or on one. It's not uncommon for a person to reach down to the ground and suddenly be bitten. If a copperhead feels threatened, it will attack.

MEDICAL MIRACLE

Southern copperhead venom contains an enzyme that attacks cancer cells. It is called contortrostatin.

This component of copperhead venom attacks certain types of cancer cells in mice, while ignoring healthy cells. Copperhead venom kills its prey, but one day it may help save humans.

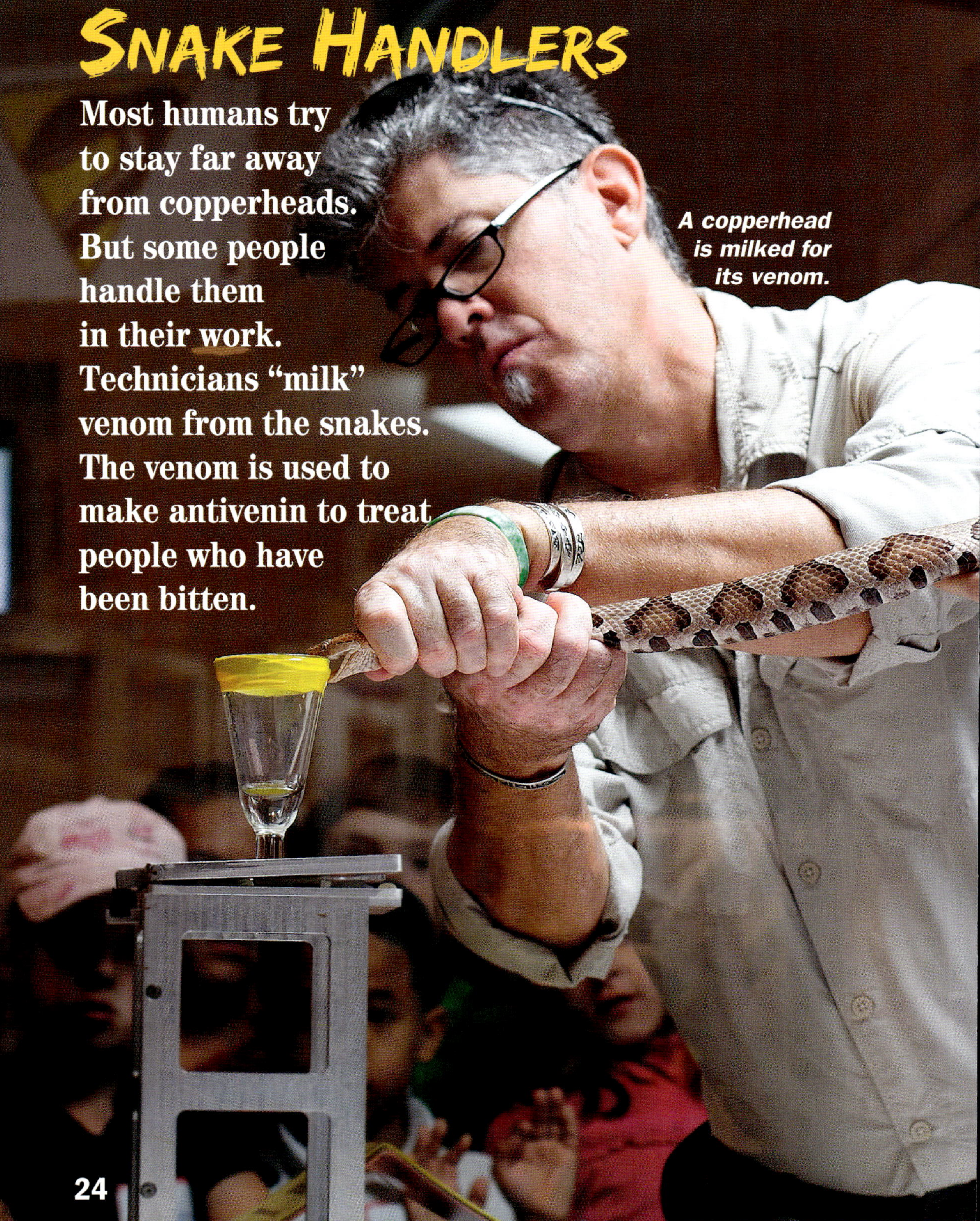

Snake Handlers

Most humans try to stay far away from copperheads. But some people handle them in their work. Technicians "milk" venom from the snakes. The venom is used to make antivenin to treat people who have been bitten.

Wildlife removal experts are trained to capture and take away dangerous pests, such as snakes. Herpetologists go to college to learn about reptiles and amphibians. They work for zoos and museums, as well as companies that do research and environmental studies.

If You Are Bitten

If you are bitten by a copperhead, it is important to follow these steps:

1) Get medical help IMMEDIATELY. Go right away, but walk. Get to a hospital quickly.

2) Stay calm. This keeps the heart from beating fast and spreading the venom through the body.

3) Look at the snake's markings or get a picture of it. If you can identify what type of snake it is, doctors will know what antivenin to use.

4) Remove any tight clothing or jewelry, such as rings or watches. Swelling begins right away and your skin needs to be able to stretch.

The best defense against a copperhead bite is to NOT get bitten. If you are in places where there are copperheads, be very aware of your surroundings. Watch where you are stepping or reaching. Wear hiking boots and loose pants to keep a snake's fangs from reaching you. Hike with a buddy, so he or she can get help if you can't hike out.

Are They Endangered?

Copperheads are a fairly common snake and are listed as "Least Concern" on the IUCN (International Union for Conservation of Nature) species list. However, loss of habitat has made northern copperheads listed as endangered in the states of Iowa and Massachusetts.

Copperheads are important for keeping down rodent populations and maintaining a balanced ecosystem. Humans need to be aware of these dangerous but beautiful snakes as they share their world with them.

GLOSSARY

AMBUSH
A surprise attack by something hiding nearby.

ANTIVENIN
Also called antivenom. A liquid used to treat and stop the effects of a bite from venomous creatures, such as snakes. Antivenin is created by injecting an animal or eggs with a small amount of a specific snake's venom. The host animal produces antibodies against the venom, which can then be taken from its blood and used to treat humans.

CAMOUFLAGE
Coloring and/or physical appearance that allows a creature to blend in with its surroundings.

COLD-BLOODED
An animal whose body temperature is the same as its surrounding environment. Reptiles, fish, amphibians, and insects are cold-blooded.

ECOSYSTEM
A biological community of animals, plants, and bacteria that live together in the same physical or chemical environment.

HEMOTOXIN

A substance, such as copperhead venom, that attacks a victim's blood and organs. Once injected into the body, a hemotoxin destroys red blood cells and the body's tissues and organs. It is painful and can kill in a short time.

PREDATOR

A creature that preys on other creatures.

RAPTORS

Birds of prey that eat meat. Raptors include eagles, falcons, hawks, owls, and vultures. Some raptors eat copperheads.

SPECIES

A group of plants or animals that are related to one another. They look alike and may produce offspring.

VENOM

A poisonous liquid that some reptiles such as snakes, Gila monsters, and scorpions use for killing prey, and for defense.

ONLINE RESOURCES

To learn more about copperheads, visit abdobooklinks.com. These links are routinely monitored and updated to provide the most current information available.

Index

Osage Copperhead